DISCOVER AND DO!

# FORCES

Written by Jane Lacey

Enslow PUBLISHING

Published in 2023 by Enslow Publishing, LLC
29 East 21st Street, New York, NY 10010



**Editor:** Katie Dicker
**Designer:** Clare Nicholas
**Series Designer:** Rocket Design (East Anglia) Ltd



Manufactured in the United States of America

CPSIA compliance information: Batch #CSENS23: For further information contact
Enslow Publishing LLC, New York, New York at 1-800-398-2504.

Please visit our website, www.enslowpublishing.com. For a free color catalog of all our high-quality books,
call toll free 1-800-398-2504 or fax 1-877-980-4454.

Cataloging-in-Publication Data
Names: Lacey, Jane.

Title: Forces / Jane Lacey.

Description: New York : Enslow Publishing, 2023. | Series: Discover and do! | Includes glossary and index.
Identifiers: ISBN 9781978530584 (pbk.) | ISBN 9781978530607 (library bound) | ISBN 9781978530591 (6pack) | ISBN 9781978530614 (ebook)

Subjects: LCSH: Force and energy--Juvenile literature.

Classification: LCC QC73.4 L334 2023 | DDC 531.6--dc23

**Picture credits:**

t=top b=bottom m=middle l=left r=right

Shutterstock: Nikolay Klimenko cover/title page l, Agor2012 cover/title page r, ProStockStudio 4, 26b and 31t, kulyk 5tl, 20m and 31b, My Portfolio 5tr and 20br, Misha Mishchenko 5b and 18m, NotionPic 6r, Macrovector 7b, DRogatnev 8m, Aleksangel 10tl and 28t, UncleFredDesign 10m, VectorShow 10tr, B Antonio 11t, NEILRAS 12b, Miro Kovacevic 13t, Dzianis_Rakhuba 14b and 16m, MaLiko 16t, VectorPlotnikoff 18b, Denis Belitsky 18t, Julija Sapic 20t, ArtMarkova 21t, ivandivandelen 22br, Satenik Guzhanina 22t and 30b, MicroOne 23t, intararit 24m, Elzloy 24t, Fuga 26tl and 29t, BabLab 27t; Getty: Art-Y 6l, MsEli 6b, Pollyana Ventura 7t, omgimages 8t, Lyudinka 8b and 29b, 3DSculptor 9t and 32, Ekaterina Zirina 10b, JoeLena 12t and 30t, 81a/Photolibrary 14t, jamielawton 15t, Vect0r0vich 16b, dan_prat 17t, nidwlw 19t, studiogstock 19tm, AnnaViolet 22ml, axel2001 24b, Mykyta Dolmatov 25t and 31m, Ales-A 26t.

All design elements from Shutterstock.

Craft models from a previous series by Q2AMedia.

DISCOVER AND DO!

# FORCES

Written by Jane Lacey

Enslow PUBLISHING

# CONTENTS

Words that appear in **bold** can be found in the glossary on pages 28–29.

# WHAT ARE FORCES?

**Forces are pushes and pulls. Forces make things move or they change the way that things move. Nothing can move without a force to push or pull it.**

## Invisible forces

You can't see a force, but you can see or feel the effect that it has. When you write with a pencil or push a door closed, you are using a force. Forces can have an effect on you too. When you bang your elbow, you feel the force as a sharp pain!

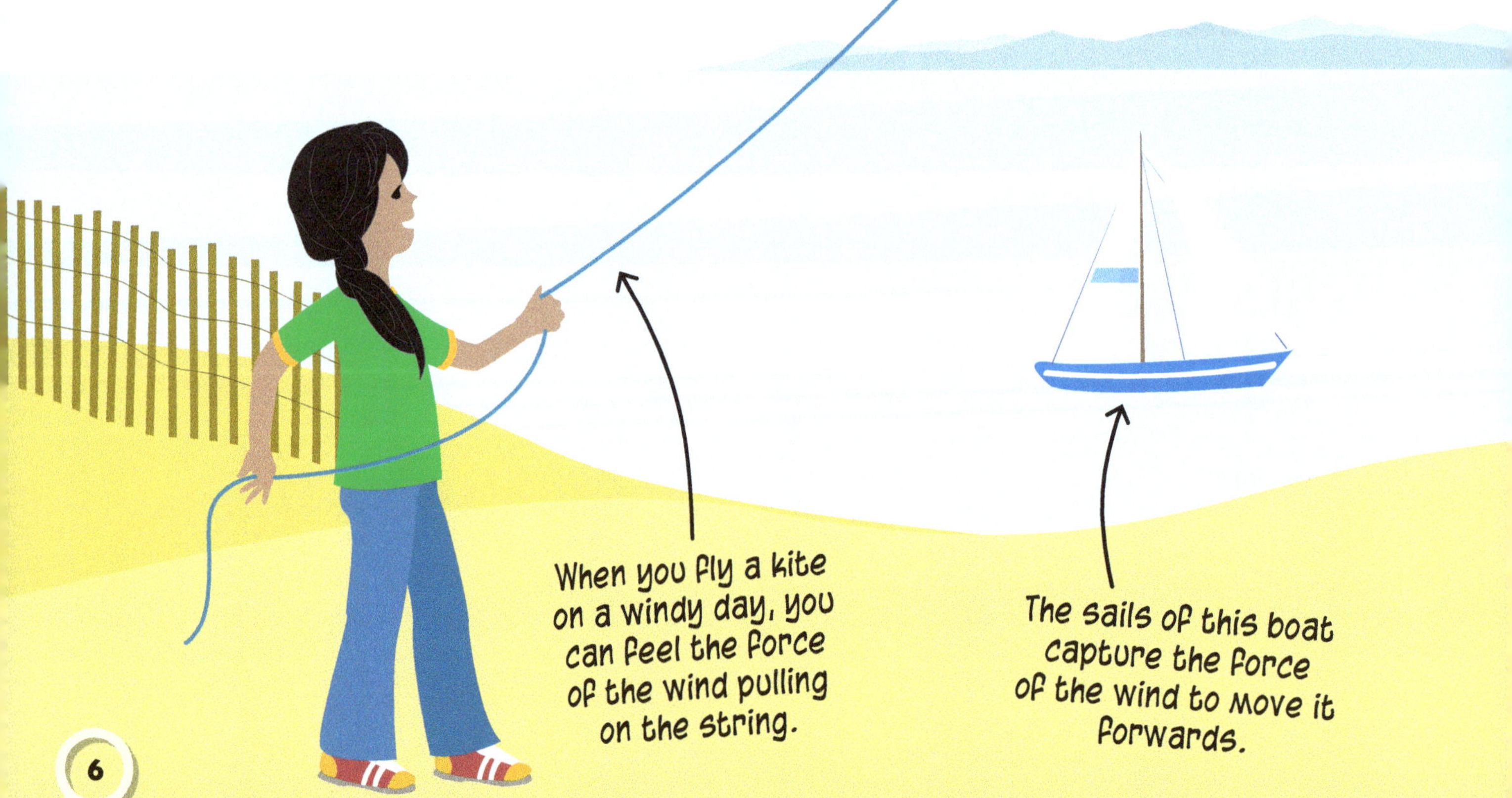

When you fly a kite on a windy day, you can feel the force of the wind pulling on the string.

The sails of this boat capture the force of the wind to move it forwards.

## What forces do

A force makes an object move in some way. When you hit a tennis ball, a force causes the ball to change direction. When you squeeze some modeling clay, a force changes the shape of the clay. The brakes on a bicycle use a force called **friction** to make the wheels slow down.

Your kick is the force that pushes a soccer ball and makes it move or change its direction.

## Machines

Forces can be very useful in our lives. **Machines**, for example, use forces to help us do work. Machines can be very simple, like a screwdriver, or complicated, like a car, but they all use forces to help make our work easier. A washing machine uses forces to move our clothes around and around, for example, to save us from having to scrub them clean.

A bike is a machine that helps us to travel. Its wheels, pedals, and brakes use different types of force.

# PUSHES AND PULLS

**A push is the opposite of a pull. You pull things toward you and you push things away from you. You pull to lift up a bag and you push a shopping cart along.**

When the forces become unbalanced in a game of tug-of-war, the stronger team pulls the other team over!

## Opposite forces

Forces usually work in pairs by pushing or pulling in opposite directions at the same time. When you sit on a chair, your body pushes down on the chair but the chair pushes back with an equal force. However, if the chair is broken, you may fall to the ground because the forces become unbalanced.

A stroller can be pushed, pulled, or turned, depending on the direction you need to go.

# Rockets

Sometimes forces are used to power things. When a rocket's engine burns **fuel**, it pushes hot gases downward with a very strong force. This creates an equal force in the opposite direction that pushes the rocket upward into space.

A force is pushing this rocket away from Earth into space.

## ACTIVITY

### MAKE A BALLOON ROCKET

**You will need:**

- **long balloon**
- **tape**
- **large drinking straw**
- **string**

1. Blow up the balloon and pinch the end to stop the air from escaping.
2. Ask a friend to help tape the straw firmly to the side of the balloon, then thread the straw onto the string.

3. Ask your friend to tie one end of the string to the back of a chair (or a door handle). Pull the other end of the string so the string is tight.

4. Count down from 10 to 0.. Let go of the balloon and shout, "LIFT OFF!"

As the air is pushed out of the back of the balloon, it pushes the balloon forwards and the balloon travels along the string.

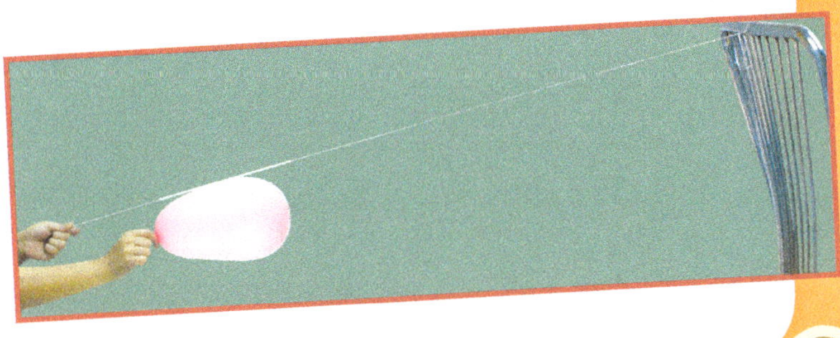

# MOVING

**Forces can make things move in any direction. When your racket hits a tennis ball, it pushes the ball away from you. When the other player hits the ball, it changes direction and comes back toward you.**

A collision has stopped these toy cars from moving.

## Slow down and stop

Once a push makes something (such as a toy car) move, it keeps moving until another force makes it stop. The toy car will stop when it bumps into an obstacle, such as a wall, which pushes in the opposite direction.

## Around and around

When an object spins around and around, it creates a force called a **centrifugal force**. A centrifugal force pulls the object outward. If you swing a ball on a string around and around, you can feel the ball pulling outward.

On this fair ride, a centrifugal force pulls the seats outward as they spin around.

**ACTIVITY**

### MAKE A SPIN DRYER

*Ask an adult to help you with this activity.*

**You will need:**

- **paper cup**
- **sharp pencil**
- **wet cloth**
- **long piece of string**

1. Ask an adult to help you make two small holes just below the rim of the cup and several holes around the cup itself (press a sharp pencil point through from the outside).
2. Tie each end of the piece of string through the two holes below the rim of the cup to make a long handle.

3. Put a very wet cloth into the cup.
4. Go outside. Hold the string and spin the cup around and around your body.

A centrifugal force will make the cup pull away from you, throw water out of the holes and spin-dry the cloth.

# GRAVITY AND WEIGHT

**Gravity** is a force that pulls everything toward the center of Earth. Gravity makes it seem as if things always fall downward. It holds us onto Earth and stops us from flying off into space!

When trees lose their leaves, the force of gravity pulls them downward.

## Weight

Objects have **weight** because gravity pulls on them. The more there is of something, the greater the pull of gravity on it and the more it weighs. A piece of **solid** soap, for example, is heavier than a sponge full of holes, even though they are about the same size.

Rivers flow downhill, tumbling over cliffs and creating waterfalls because of the force of gravity.

# Center of gravity

The center of gravity is the point where the weight of something balances. Everything has a center of gravity. If you wear a heavy backpack you will find that your center of gravity changes. You will need to balance more carefully when you move around.

These pots balance because their center of gravity is positioned over the women's heads.

## ACTIVITY

### MAKE A BALANCING BEAR

**You will need:**

- **stiff card stock**
- **pencils and crayons**
- **scissors**
- **2 small coins (of the same size)**
- **glue**
- **stick**

1. Draw two copies of this balancing bear about 4 inches (10 cm) tall on stiff card stock and cut them out.

2. Decorate the shapes so one is the back of the bear and the other is the front.

3. Stick the small coins to the back of the "hand" paws on one copy and stick the undecorated sides together.

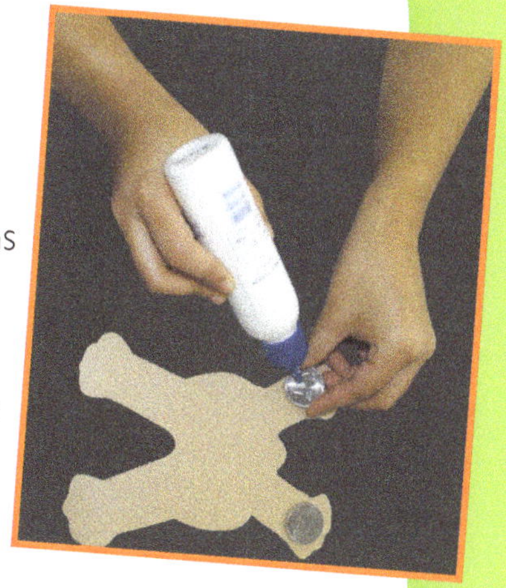

4. Balance the bear's nose downward on the end of a pencil or a stick.

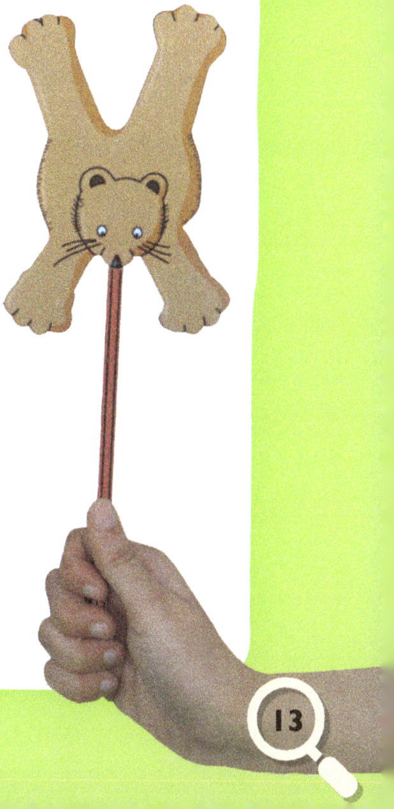

The bear will balance because the weight of the coins makes its nose the center of gravity.

# FLOATING AND SINKING

**When you put a solid object in water, it is pulled down by the force of gravity, and pushed up by a force called upthrust. The strength of these forces affects the way the object moves.**

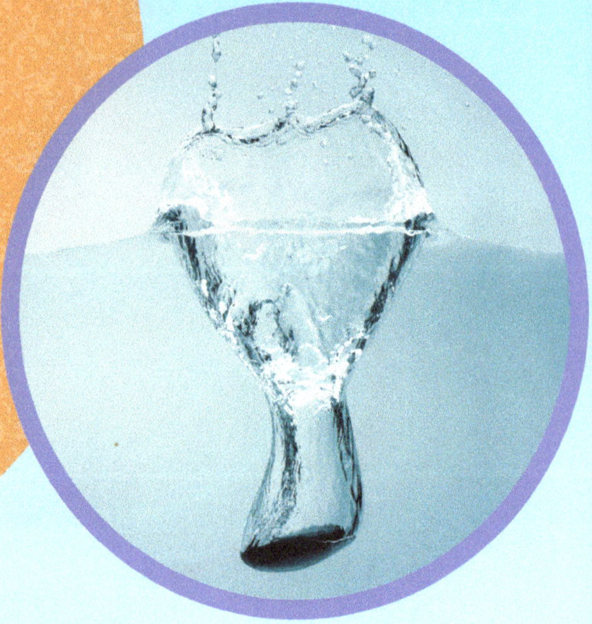

A tiny pebble sinks because it is heavy for its size.

## Weight and size

An object will either **float** or **sink** depending on its shape, its size, and the **material** it is made of. Things that are light for their size will float. Things that are heavy for their size will sink.

This ship and iceberg float because they have a large surface area. They are full of air spaces that make them light for their size.

# Upthrust

Some solid objects float on water because of the force of upthrust. When a boat pushes down on the water, the water pushes up with a force too. If the water pushes up with the same amount of force, the boat will float.

An inner tube floats and carries your weight because the water pushes it back up!

## ACTIVITY

## GUESS THE FLOATING SHAPES

**You will need:**

- **8 pieces of modeling clay (weighed to check they are the same weight)**
- **bowl of water**

1. Make some different clay shapes, such as a ball, a sausage, a flat shape, a boat, a bowl, and a cone.

2. Guess if the shape will float or sink. Try it out. Were you right?

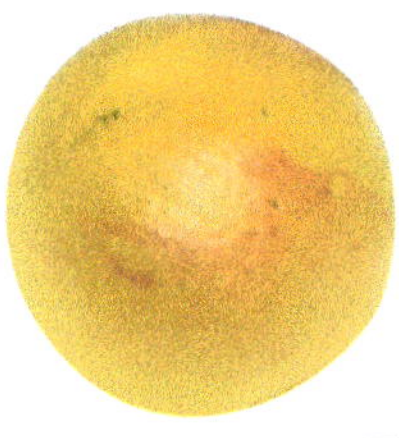

3. Make a chart to record your findings.

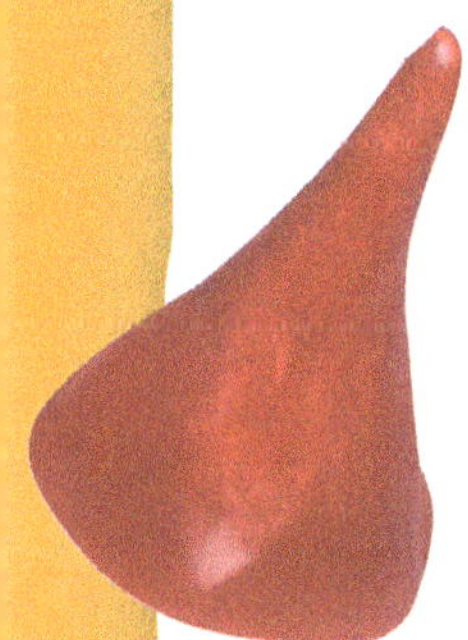

| | My guess: Float | My guess: Sink | Float | Sink |
|---|---|---|---|---|
| Ball shape | | ✓ | | ✓ |
| Sausage shape | | | | |
| Bowl shape | | | | |

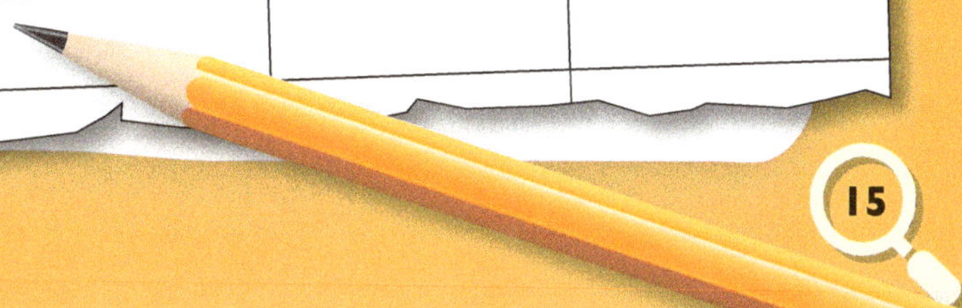

# FRICTION

**Things rubbing together create a force called friction. When you move sandpaper against wood, the rough surfaces get caught on each other. Ice skates glide with less friction because the ice is smooth.**

Ice skates have thin, metal blades that glide across the smooth surface of an ice rink.

## Slowing down

If you push a book along a table, it travels a short way and then slows down. It eventually stops because of the friction caused by the book and the table rubbing together. Friction slows the book down because the force works in the opposite direction to the way the book is moving.

Friction can be useful. Hiking boots have patterned soles that rub against the ground to stop you from slipping.

# Floating on air

When a boat moves through water, the water rubs against its sides, creating friction and slowing it down. A **hovercraft** moves more quickly because it travels on a cushion of air that creates less friction with the water.

A hovercraft has a large fan that creates a cushion of air to lift it off the water.

ACTIVITY

## MAKE A HOVERCRAFT

**You will need:**

- **water bottle drinking spout (with valve)**
- **strong glue**
- **blank/old CD**
- **balloon**

1. Shut the bottle's spout valve and glue it to the center of the CD.

2. Blow up the balloon and pull the end over the spout.

3. Hold the balloon end over the valve with one hand and carefully pull up the spout (hidden under the balloon end) to open it and force air downward out of the balloon.

4. Watch the CD move across the floor on a cushion of air. Now push your hovercraft and feel the friction between the CD and the floor.

5. Blow up the balloon and make your hovercraft hover again!

# DRAG

**Moving boats, planes, and cars are slowed down by water and air rubbing against them. This makes a kind of friction called resistance or drag.**

The streamlined shape of this plane helps it to fly faster.

## Streamlined shapes

Smooth, pointed, **streamlined** shapes cut through air and water and help to reduce drag. A jet plane and a speedboat have streamlined shapes to speed through air and water. A helicopter and a trailer do not have such streamlined shapes, so they move more slowly.

A shark's streamlined shape helps to reduce drag as it moves quickly through the water.

# Falling

A parachute is designed to give a slow, soft landing. The curved shape of the parachute creates resistance as it falls through the air, slowing it down. The bigger the parachute, the more air is trapped and the slower it falls.

Gravity pulls the parachutist down, but the parachute creates drag so it floats down slowly.

ACTIVITY

## MAKE A PARACHUTE

**You will need:**

- **large paper plate**
- **hole punch**
- **paints**
- **4 equal lengths of string**
- **small plastic toys**

1. Punch four holes at equal distances around the edge of the plate. This will be your parachute canopy.

2. Paint your canopy with bright colors. When it's dry, tie one end of each piece of string through the four holes.

3. Tie the other ends of the string to your toy. Drop the parachute and watch it float down.

What happens when you drop toys of different sizes?

# ELASTICITY

**Things that are made of elastic material, such as rubber bands, stretchy socks, sponges, and rubber balls, have a force called elasticity. When you stretch or squeeze them and then let go, they snap back into shape.**

## Springs

A spring is a long piece of wire or plastic coiled around and around. When you press down on or stretch a spring and let it go, it springs back into its original shape. Springs are hidden inside all kinds of things we use every day, such as scales, staplers, and clothes pins.

When a weight is added to some kitchen scales, a spring is pressed down and turns the measuring dial.

The coiled spring of this Slinky keeps trying to go back to its original shape.

# Faster and higher

Elastic and springs can be used to shoot objects fast through the air or along the ground, such as with a catapult, or make something bounce up and down, like a trampoline.

The springs on a trampoline let you bounce higher than you can by jumping up and down on the ground.

ACTIVITY

## MAKE A CAR CATAPULT

*Ask an adult to help you with this activity.*

**You will need:**

- **one piece of wood 8 inches x 1.5 inches (20 cm x 4 cm)**
- **two pieces of wood about 8 inches x 0.75 inch (20 cm x 2 cm)**
- **4 nails**
- **hammer**
- **strong, long rubber band**
- **toy car**

1. Ask an adult to make a three-sided frame by nailing the pieces of wood together. Ask them to hammer a nail partly into the open ends.

2. Loop the ends of the rubber band around each nail and place the frame on a flat surface.

3. Put the back of the toy car against the rubber band and push it back. Let go and watch the elastic force push the car along!

How could you make the car go faster and further?

# MAGNETISM

**Magnetism** is a force that pulls and pushes objects without actually touching them. A magnet pulls and pushes things using the force of magnetism.

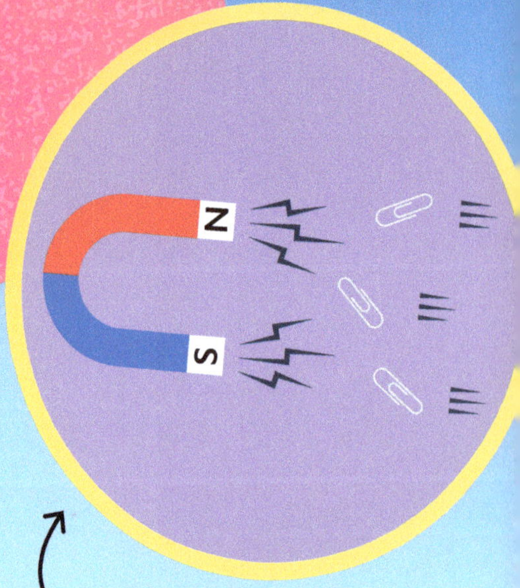


Steel paper clips are attracted to this magnet because steel contains iron.

## Magnetic materials

Magnets **attract,** or pull magnetic materials toward them. Some metals, such as iron, cobalt, and nickel, are magnetic materials. Magnets will not attract non-magnetic materials such as glass, wood, and plastic.

Giant electromagnets are used in scrapyards to pick up magnetic materials. They drop the materials when the **electricity** is turned off.

## Poles

Like the Earth, bar magnets have a north and south **pole**. One end is the south pole (usually blue), the other end is the north pole (usually red). Opposite poles attract each other and the same poles **repel,** or push each other away.

The same poles of two bar magnets will push away from each other.

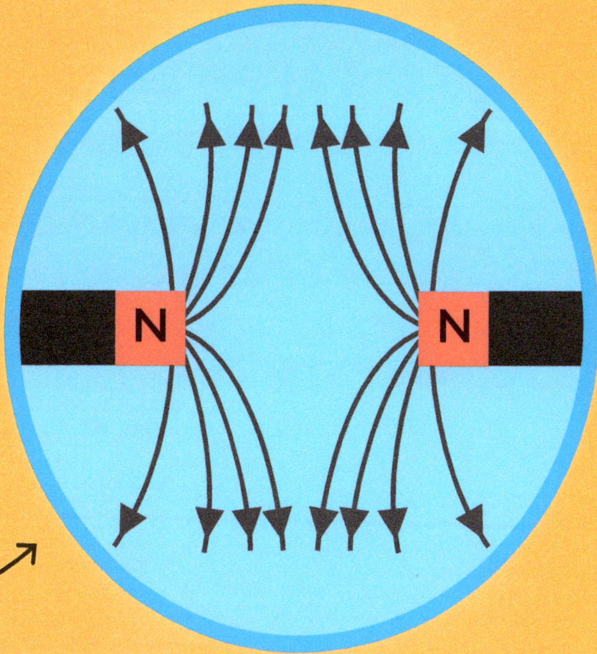


ACTIVITY

## TREASURE HUNT

**You will need:**

- **tray of sand**
- **model trees and animals**
- **small metal objects**
- **strong horseshoe magnet**
- **sticker labels**
- **pen**

1. Add the model trees and animals to the sand to make it look like a treasure island.

2. Use the horseshoe magnet to test some small metal objects–such as paper clips, nails, keys, spoons, small metal toys–for magnetism.

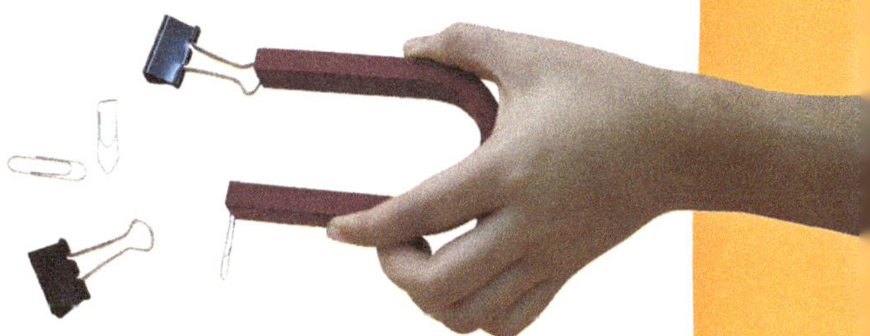

3. Write money values onto the labels. Stick them to the objects and ask someone else to bury the objects in the sand.

4. With a friend, take turns finding the objects with the magnet. The winner is the one whose objects add up to the highest value.

# USING FORCES

**We use forces every time we use a machine. Some machines, such as cars, need fuel to work. Other machines use electricity. Levers and pulleys are simple machines that don't need to use fuel or electricity.**

You use a lever to open a drink can.

## Levers

A lever is a rod that makes lifting easier. When you push down on a spoon handle to open a can, you are using the spoon as a lever to help you lift the lid. A lever needs something to **pivot** on, such as the edge of the can. Your arm is also a lever. It pivots around your elbow.

A seesaw is a type of lever. It pivots on a point in the middle to lift and lower people sitting at either end.

# Pulleys

A pulley is a machine that helps us to lift things. It has a rope running around one or more wheels. Pulling down on the rope makes it much easier to lift a heavy object attached to the other end of the rope. The more wheels the rope goes around, the easier it is to lift the **load**.

This crane uses a system of pulleys to lift huge, heavy crates.

## ACTIVITY

### MAKE A PULLEY

**You will need:**

- **large empty spool (from a spool of ribbon or string)**
- **dowel (thin wooden rod) about 20 inches (50 cm) long**
- **bag of fruit**
- **string about 6 feet (1.8 m) long**

1. Thread the dowel through the spool.
2. Ask a friend to hold each end of the dowel as high and as firmly as they can.

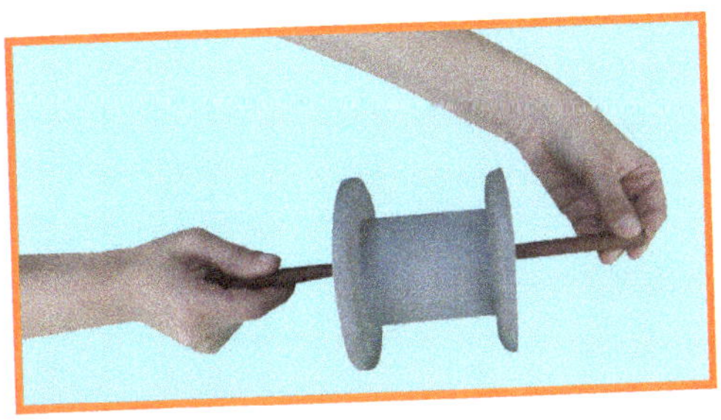

3. Tie one end of the string to the bag of fruit and run the other end over the spool.
4. Pull down on the free end of the string to lift the bag of fruit.

Now try lifting the fruit by the string without using the pulley. Which is easier?

# WIND AND WATER

**Moving air and water create forces that can be used to make things move. Wind is moving air. It pushes a kite and keeps it flying. Surfers ride the water using the force of big waves.**

The power in this wave moves the surfboard along.

Wind turbines turn because of the power of the wind, and they generate electricity.

## Wind power

Wind power can be destructive. A tornado creates a force strong enough to blow down houses and trees. But wind can be useful too. Wind is a source of **energy** that will never run out.

# Water power

Water wheels have been used for centuries to power machinery, such as the millstones at a flour mill that grind grain. Today, the force of flowing water is used at **hydroelectric power stations** to create electricity.

Flowing water turns a water wheel to power the machinery at this mill.

## ACTIVITY

## MAKE A WATER WHEEL

**You will need:**

- **large paper plate**
- **pencil**
- **ruler**
- **scissors**
- **sticky tack**
- **fine string**
- **faucet**
- **small plastic toy**

1. Cut out the inner circle of the paper plate and copy this template onto it using a pencil and a ruler. Cut down the solid lines to about 0.75 inch (2 cm) from the center and fold back the dotted lines.

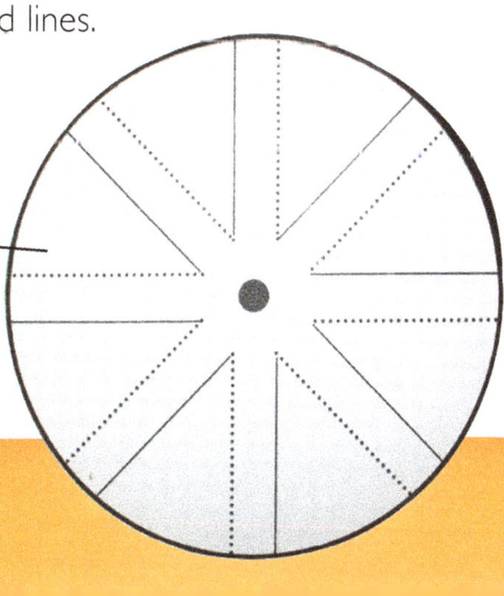

Template

2. Push the pencil through the center of the wheel and hold it in place with sticky tack on either side of the hole.

3. Tie the string to one end of the pencil and attach a small toy to the loose end. Turn a faucet on to a light flow. Balance the pencil on your fingers under the water to turn the wheel and lift the toy.

# Glossary

## attract

To attract is to pull objects nearer.

## centrifugal force

A centrifugal force pulls an object going around in a circle outwards and away from the center of the circle.

## drag

Drag is a force that slows down moving objects.

## elasticity

Elasticity allows materials that have stretched to snap back to their original size and shape.

## electricity

Electricity is a type of energy that gives machines the power to work.

## energy

Energy is the power that makes things work.

## float

To float is to stay on the surface of the water and not sink.

## friction

Friction is a force created when surfaces rub against each other.

## fuel

Fuel is something that is burned for energy. For example, gas gives a car the energy to move. Food gives us energy to work and play.

## gravity

Gravity is a force that pulls objects toward the center of Earth. Gravity gives objects weight.

## hovercraft

A hovercraft is a kind of boat that moves across water on a cushion of air.

## hydroelectric power station

A hydroelectric power station produces electricity by using energy from running water.

## lever

A lever is a rod used as a tool to make lifting easier.

## load

A load is something big or heavy that is carried.

## machine

A machine makes our work easier. For example, a hand whisk makes whisking eggs easier. A washing machine makes washing clothes easier.

**magnetism**

Magnetism is a force that attracts objects made from some kinds of metal, particularly iron.

**material**

A material is a substance, such as metal or wood, that is used to make the objects around us.

**pivot**

To pivot is to turn or rotate around a fixed point.

**pole**

A pole is either end of a bar magnet, where the magnetic field is strongest.

**pulley**

A pulley is a rope running around one or more wheels that helps us to lift things.

**repel**

To repel is to push objects away.

**resistance**

Resistance is a force that slows down an object that is moving.

**sink**

To sink is to go underneath the water and not stay floating on the surface.

**solid**

A solid object has a shape of its own. It is not a liquid or a gas.

**streamlined**

A streamlined shape moves easily through air or water.

**upthrust**

Upthrust is a force that pushes up on things that are floating in water.

**weight**

Weight is the force with which an object is attracted to Earth by the pull of gravity.

# Quiz

**1 Bicycle brakes use which force?**

a) a magnetic force
b) a frictional force
c) a gravitational force
d) an electric force

**2 Forces work in pairs by pushing or pulling:**

a) up at the same time
b) down at the same time
c) in opposite directions at the same time
d) in the same direction at the same time

**3 Forces can make things move:**

a) in any direction
b) in one direction
c) up and down
d) back and forth

**4 A centrifugal force pulls objects:**

a) inward
b) outward
c) backward
d) forward

**5 Objects have weight because:**

a) they are big
b) they are solid
c) they are heavy
d) gravity pulls on them

**6 A parachute has a curved shape:**

a) to make the parachutist less heavy
b) to make the parachutist spin around
c) because it creates air resistance
d) because it looks pretty

**7 Which of the following objects have a spring?**

a) a kitchen scale
b) a clothes pin
c) a stapler
d) a door handle

**8 Which is NOT a magnetic material?**

a) iron
b) cobalt
c) nickel
d) glass

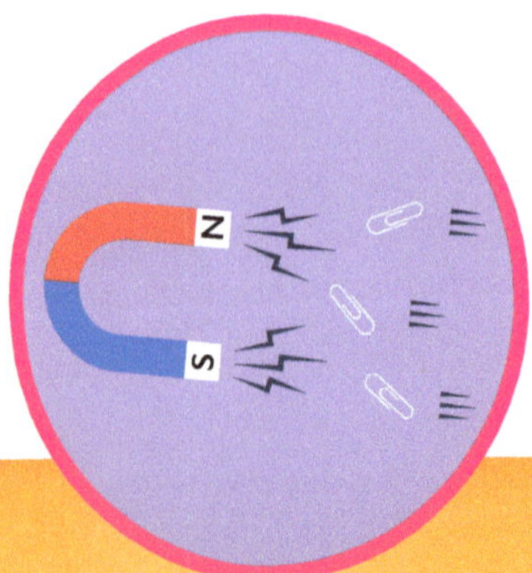

**9** **A pulley is a machine that helps you to:**

a) lift things
b) turn things
c) pull things
d) push things

**10** **Which CAN'T be used to create electricity?**

a) the power of the wind
b) the power of flowing water
c) the movement of a turbine
d) the movement of a kite

**ANSWERS** 1b, 2c, 3a, 4b, 5d, 6c, 7 they all do!, 8d, 9a, 10d

# FURTHER INFORMATION

## BOOKS

*A Question of Science: Why doesn't the moon fall down?* by Anna Claybourne, Wayland

*Be a Scientist: Investigating Forces* by Jacqui Bailey, Wayland

*Boom Science: Forces* by Georgia Amson-Bradshaw, Franklin Watts

*100% Get the Whole Picture: Forces and Matter* by Paul Mason, Wayland

## WEBSITES

**Learn about different types of forces:** www.bbc.co.uk/bitesize/topics/znmmn39

**Try your hand at some force experiments:** www.fizzicseducation.com.au/category/150-science-experiments/force-movement-experiments

**Look at the amazing work of pulleys in action:** learning.sciencemuseumgroup.org.uk/resources/can-you-lift-something-heavier-than-yourself

**Forces: Some questions and answers:** www.pbs.org/video/science-trek-force-and-motion

# Index